NEW ATKINS DIET PLAN 2019-20

The Ultimate Diet for Beginners and Step by Step Simpler Way to Lose Weight | New Atkins Diet Revolution

DR BRANDON J HEARN

TABLE OF CONTENTS

Introduction

Before starting the popular Atkins weight loss program, there are some important questions you should ask. How does the Atkins diet work? And does the Atkins diet work if you want to lose weight and keep the pounds off for good?

The Atkins plan has undergone significant changes in recent years. If you are considering the diet, use this guide to see if the plan is right for you and if you want to lose weight.

Atkins is one of the most recognized low carbohydrate diets. Developed by Dr. Robert Atkins in the 1970s, the original version of the weight loss program was heavily criticized in the early years because it included relatively high levels of saturated fat and protein. But since then, the popularity of low-carb diets has exploded, and newer versions of the Atkins plan have gained acceptance in many, but not all, weight loss groups.

Dieters who use the current Atkins plan are learning to count net carbs to lose weight. The traditional Atkins plan has four stages:

- Induction phase. For two weeks or longer, dieters keep their net carbs at the lowest level.

- Balancing Phase. Dieters slowly add grams of net carbs to find the best carbohydrate balance.
- Fine Tuning Phase. Dieters make small tweaks to reach and maintain their target weight for at least a month.
- Lifetime maintenance. Dieters continue to eat a healthy diet with limited carbohydrates to maintain their target weight.

The best plan for you

The Atkins program includes two plans for different types of dieters.

Atkins 20:

The Atkins 20 plan is what most people would consider to be the classic Atkins plan. Dieters on this program start off by consuming only 20 net carbs per day. Dieters eat a variety of approved (basic) vegetables, lean meats, cheeses and healthy fats to meet their energy needs. After two weeks at Atkins 20, dieters start adding berries and nuts in five net carb steps. Then they gradually learn to incorporate more healthy carbohydrate choices to reach and maintain their target weight.

Atkins 40:

This plan provides a more relaxed program where dieters eat from all food groups from day one. The plan is designed for people who have 40 pounds or less to lose. Dieters start the first phase of the plan by consuming 40 grams of net carbs a day from vegetables, fruits, nuts, legumes and whole grains. As dieters approach their target weight, they add carbs in 10 net carb steps to find their personal carb "sweet spot" to maintain their healthy weight.

No diet works for everyone. The key is to find a diet that fits your lifestyle so you can stick to it enough to reach your goals and preserve your new body. It you choose the Atkins diet, these are a few things to expect.

- Portion control. Contrary to popular belief, part control is built into the Atkins system. So plan not to binge on steak, butter, cheese and bacon for weeks to lose weight. Dieters on the Atkins 40 plan, for example, are reminded to eat three 4 to 6 ounce servings of protein each day and only 2 to 4 servings of fat each day.

- Limited alcohol. Drinking alcohol is not recommended during the first few weeks on the Atkins plan. So as you go through the plan, alcohol should be limited to reaching and maintaining your target weight.
- Counts net carbs. You don't have to count calories on the Atkins plan, but you do need to count net carbs. For some people, this process can be too tedious because calculating netcarbs takes a little work. But the Atkins website and easy-to-use app make it easier to find the numbers.
- Carb withdrawal. Because the typical American diet is full of carbohydrates, reducing carbs to lose weight can be challenging. Some dieters complain of headaches, low energy and poor mood in the early stages of the diet.
- Quick results. Because the induction phase of the Atkins diet is (for most) a drastic change in their typical diet, those who follow the diet tend to lose inches and weight quickly in the early stages of this plan. Critics of the diet, however, will argue that this early stage is too difficult to follow.

Of course, any dieter can go low carb without going on Atkins. But according to one expert, Atkins provides a structure that helps dieters lose more weight. "Dieters have a choice and they can either turn to a low carbohydrate diet or try to do it on their own," says Marie Spano, MS, RD, CSCS, CSSD. Marie is a nutritionist who has done work on behalf of Atkins. She says that "having a program to follow can provide guidance, suggestions, recipe ideas, and an online community of people working toward the same goal. Atkins is a leader in low carbohydrate diets and they have helped people lose weight with various versions of low carbohydrate diets for over 40 years."

To deal with constipation

Some dieters complain of constipation during Atkin's induction. While this condition does not happen to everyone, there are a few things you can do to reduce constipation during induction and a few steps you can take to prevent it.

First, make sure you drink plenty of water during this first phase of the Atkins plan. Program experts recommend that you drink at least eight 8-ounce glasses a day. Next, watch your intake of caffeine. While you are allowed to drink beverages such as black coffee or tea, caffeine may seem like a diuretic. So you can get dehydrated when you drink too much of it and get constipated as a result.

Then choose your limited carbohydrates carefully. Eating healthy carbs with fiber will promote healthy digestion and feces. Atkins recommends eating at least 12-15 daily grams of carbohydrate from lettuce greens and other vegetables.

Finally, if you experience constipation during Atkin's induction, the program recommends that you "mix one tablespoon or more of psyllium shells in one cup or more of water and drink daily. Or mix ground flaxseed in a shake or sprinkle wheat bran on a salad or vegetable."

Does it work in the long run?

The Atkins diet has been studied extensively over the years. Other low carbohydrate diets have also been studied, most often compared to moderate or high carbohydrate plans. Many studies show a modest weight loss with Atkins in the long term as long as dieters stick to the plan. But sticking to the diet can be difficult for many people.

So should you try the Atkins diet to lose weight? Authors of several recent diet studies often come to the same conclusion: Choose any plan you want to stick to. The difference between one diet and another is not big enough to determine that a single diet is the perfect solution for weight loss. Assess your lifestyle and personal preferences to find a diet that you can live with and maintain for life.

The Atkins Diet

This diet is named after its inventor Robert Atkins and is based on the low-carb principle, or Robert Atkins is the inventor of this diet model. The Atkins diet offers the advantage that you do not have to starve to lose weight; it just has to be done rigorously without carbohydrates. The menu includes meat, fish, eggs, and dairy products, as well as a small selection of vegetables. The fruit is not in the diet of the Atkins diet because fruit contains fructose, so carbohydrates.

For many people who want to lose weight, the Atkins diet is a good alternative to calorie-restricted diets, as the Atkins diet allows you to eat almost any amount of the permitted food. The principle of the diet is based on the assumption that for the utilization and preparation of fats carbohydrates are needed, these are absent with the food intake, the supplied fat is excreted, and also the fat burning of the body is stimulated.

The Atkins diet sparked a veritable hype in the 1980s and became the food model of the beautiful and famous in Hollywood. Many of today's low-carb diets are based on the Atkins-based principle, but many of the strict rules have been softened and, for example, not so rigorously without fruit. During the Atkins diet, sugar, desserts, pasta such as pasta and bread, as well as most fruit, must be avoided.

The principle of Atkins the diet

The Atkins diet allows protein and fat. The human body cannot store the protein, and therefore, excess amounts are eliminated. The fat, in turn, cannot be processed without the carbohydrates.

The Atkins diet is based on the assumption that carbohydrates are needed for the metabolism of fats.

If these are no longer supplied, the fat absorbed by the food can no longer be processed and is excreted. Also, the renunciation of carbohydrates leads to a change in metabolism. Carbohydrates are absorbed quickly into the blood and quickly increase blood sugar levels. By eliminating carbohydrates, the blood sugar level remains constantly low. A low blood sugar level, in turn, stimulates fat burning, which in spite of high fat intake in the Atkins diet leads to the breakdown of the stored fat reserves. This describes the state of ketosis desired in the Atkins diet.

In ketosis, ketone bodies are formed in the blood in the liver to replace the lack of glucose in the blood from the carbohydrates. For such "hunger states," the liver can extract ketone bodies from the fat reserves. So to keep the low blood sugar level at a constant level, the body relies on the processing of fat reserves. Incidentally, the ketone bodies are created in every situation in which the body has to resort to the burning of its fat reserves. A sweetish-acetone-like bad breath can recognize people with ketosis.

HEALTHY SWEETS (such as plain dark chocolate) Sparingly

RED WINE (optional)
No more than 1-2 glasses a day

TEA (white, green, oolong)
2-4 cups a day

HEALTHY HERBS & SPICES (such as garlic, ginger, turmeric, cinnamon) Unlimited amounts

OTHER SOURCES OF PROTEIN (natural cheeses, lowfat dairy, omega-3 enriched eggs, skinless poultry, lean meats) 1-2 a week

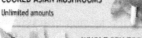

COOKED ASIAN MUSHROOMS
Unlimited amounts

WHOLE SOY FOODS (edamame, soy nuts, soymilk, tofu, tempeh) 1-2 a day

FISH & SEAFOOD (wild Alaskan salmon, Alaskan black cod, sardines) 2-6 a week

HEALTHY FATS (extra virgin olive oil, expeller-pressed canola oil, nuts - especially walnuts, avocados, seeds - including hemp seeds and freshly ground flaxseeds) 5-7 a day

WHOLE & CRACKED GRAINS 3-5 a day	PASTA (al dente) 2-3 a week	BEANS & LEGUMES 1-2 a day

SUPPLEMENTS High-quality multivitamin/multi-mineral that includes key antioxidants (vitamin C, vitamin E, mixed carotenoids, and selenium); Co-enzyme Q-10; 2-3 grams of a molecularly distilled fish oil; 1,000 IU of vitamin D3 Daily

VEGETABLES (both raw and cooked, from all parts of the color spectrum, organic when possible) 4-5 a day minimum

FRUITS (fresh in season or frozen, organic when possible) 3-4 a day

The course of the Atkins diet

The Atkins diet runs in several phases. In the initial phase of the diet is about the state of ketosis, so to achieve the combustion of their fat reserves by carbohydrate avoidance. Atkins' intake of carbohydrates has to be drastically reduced in this phase. Atkins recommended not consuming more than five grams of carbs a day, but later he withdrew that rigorous amount and allowed a maximum of 20 grams of carbohydrates a day.

Mainly overweight persons should take thereby however fewer carbohydrates, to start the fat burning as fast as possible.

The first and strictest phase of the Atkins diet was to last for several weeks. Meat, eggs, fish, cheese, and other dairy products are allowed in a sufficient amount of saturation. Atkins himself has criticized the presentation of his diet as an invitation to dine. Atkins himself suggests no large portions, but moderate and satisfying amounts, after all, the sense of this unusual diet is indeed decrease without hunger, but gluttony is not meant. Once the condition of fat burning has started without starving, the number of carbohydrates may be increased a little daily, for example, a piece of fruit.

In this **second phase** of the diet, the number of carbohydrates may be increased until the weight loss stagnates. Then the amount must be brought back to the last state, at which still a weight loss has taken place.

This **third phase** is maintained until the desired weight loss occurs. After that, the Atkins diet is by no means over. After reaching his desired weight, you can again daily increase the number of carbohydrates until the weight comes to a standstill. This diet should now be maintained permanently. Atkins himself recommends the additional intake of dietary supplements.

A typical day during the Atkins diet

Since bread is mostly taboo in the Atkins diet, breakfast is unusual for German standards. For example, a typical breakfast in the Atkins diet consists of eggs with ham or even bacon, although it may be two eggs in the pan and the bacon does not have to be lean. Unsweetened coffee or tea is allowed in any amount.

Lunch is usually mainly meat, which may be steak or meatballs. It may be a small portion of low-carbohydrate vegetables, such as broccoli or spinach.

For dinner you could, for example, take fried fish. Also, a cheese platter with associated wine is allowed in the Atkins diet.

If you like to nibble something in between and want to stick to the Atkins diet, you can eat bacon cubes or cheese cubes. Also, an egg in between is allowed.

The benefit of the Atkins diet is that you are allowed to eat your fill during meals and can also take snacks; you just have to stick to the approved food. In this direction, you are not bound to tight diet plans with an Atkins diet and can also eat at all times of the day.

Does this really work - eat and lose weight?

Atkins diet leads to weight loss. The body responds to the little blood sugar level by releasing ketone bodies from the stored fat in the liver to keep the blood sugar level constant. However, the weight loss is not overly high; average subjects lost to a study only about five kilograms within a year. And sticking to the Atkins diet is also not easy because of the lack of carbohydrates. Basic foods such as potatoes or bread are forbidden, and the abandonment of fresh fruit is difficult for many people willing to lose weight.

Criticism of the Atkins diet

The originally highly praised Atkins diet is today very controversial. This is partly due to the very one-sided diet with lots of meat and protein. The lack of fruits and vegetables inevitably leads to deficiency symptoms, so that Atkins himself recommends the intake of supplements in addition to his diet. Even a diet without a varied diet is difficult to endure, even the biggest meat lover, the 23st steak finally hungrily literally. Also, the Atkins diet is recommended only for healthy people, so before starting a visit to the doctor should take place in which the personal cardiovascular situation is checked, and the most important laboratory parameters are determined.

In particular, the kidney values must be in order because the diet for kidney patients may even be dangerous because of the high protein content.

The deliberately induced ketosis can be pointed in the form of ketoacidosis, a hyperacidity of the blood, dangerous. Today, many more balanced diets are known, which use the low-carb approach of Atkins, but allow a higher proportion of fruits and vegetables and which overall allow a gentler treatment of health than the strict Atkins diet. Those who still want to get involved in this diet should not give up the previous visit to the doctor and monitor his laboratory parameters during the diet.

The nature of the diet

The diet involves limited consumption of carbohydrates to switch the body's metabolism from metabolic glucose as energy into converting stored body fat into energy. This process, called ketosis, begins when insulin levels are low; In normal people, insulin is lowest when blood sugar is low. Reduced insulin levels induce lipolysis, which uses fat to produce ketones. On the other hand, low calorie carbohydrates affect the body by increasing blood sugar after consuming Fiber, due to its low digestibility, provides little or no food energy and does not significantly affect glucose and insulin levels.

In his early books as Dr. Atkins' New Diet Revolution, Atkins made the controversial argument that low-carbohydrate diets produce a metabolic benefit because "burning fat takes more calories so you consume more calories". He cited a study in which he estimated this benefit to be 950 calories a day. A review study published in the Lancet concluded that there was no such metabolic benefit and Dieters was simply eating fewer calories due to boredom. Astrup stated, "The monotony and simplicity of the diet could inhibit appetite and food intake".

In the recent book by Westman, Phinney, and Volek, the authors suggest optimal levels of protein, fat and calorie intake, and have moved away from the metabolic benefit theory.

The diet limits "net carbs". An effect tends to decrease the onset of hunger, perhaps due to longer duration digestion. 2002 The New Diet Revolution book that hunger is the main reason why low-fat diets fail and that the diet is easier because you are satisfied with adequate protein, fat and fiber.

Net carbohydrates can be calculated from a food source by subtracting fiber and sugar alcohols from total carbohydrates. Sugar alcohols contain about two calories per gram, although the American Diabetes Association recommends that diabetics do not count alcohol as carbohydrates. Fructose has four calories per gram but has a very low glycemic index and does not cause insulin production, probably because β-cells have low levels of GLUT5. Leptin, an appetite regulating hormone, is not triggered after ingestion of fructose. For some, this may create an unsatisfactory feeling after consumption, which may promote binge behavior that culminates in an increased blood triglyceride level as a result of fructose liver conversion.

Preferred foods in all categories are whole, unprocessed foods with a low glycemic index, although restrictions on low glycemic carbohydrates are the same as those for high glycemic carbohydrates. Atkins Dietary Supplements, the company formed to market foods that work with the diet, recommends that a maximum of 20% of calories eaten while on a diet come from saturated fat.

The Atkins Diabetes Revolution book states that for people whose blood sugar is abnormally high or who have type 2 diabetes mellitus, the Atkins Diet decreases or eliminates the need for drugs to treat these conditions. The Atkins Blood Sugar Control Program is said to be an individualized approach to weight control and permanent management of risk factors for diabetes and cardiovascular disease. The Atkins Diet is not accepted in conventional treatment for diabetes.

Ketogenic diet

The initial phase of the Atkins Diet is referred to as the induction phase and is considered a ketogenic diet. In ketogenic diets, the production of ketones contributes to the energy production in Krebs cycle. Ketogenic diets rely on insulin response to blood sugar. Insulin is a hormone that produces beta cells in the pancreas in response to high levels of blood glucose. The main function of insulin is to shuttle glucose from the blood to peripheral tissues where they will be needed for fuel or stored as fat. Thus insulin is a regulator of blood glucose that is too high.

17

Because ketogenic dieters eat few carbohydrates, there is no glucose that can trigger insulin response. Therefore, the body must seek an alternative fuel source to meet its metabolic needs. During this diet, the main sources of fuel for human cells are now at less than adequate supply, cells must take alternative steps to convert stored fuel into glucose. Other than carbohydrate intake, the cells must depend on glucose production from the conversion of either protein or stored fat.

When blood levels of glucose are low, hormones are released to signal the need to raise blood sugar. This is in contrast to the actions of insulin. Since the body is less able to compensate for a state of hypoglycemia than it is for hyperglycemia, hormones released causing a cascade result in glycogen release from the liver and adipose tissue cell conversion of triacylglycerol to fatty acids.

Blood glucose levels need to drop to less than 3.58 mmol / L for growth hormone, adrenaline and glucagon to be released to maintain energy metabolism. In the fat cells, growth hormone and adrenaline initiate triacylglycerol is divided into fatty acids. These fatty acids go to the liver and muscles, where they must be oxidized and give acetyl-CoA, which is a part of the cancer cycle directly. However, the excess acetyl-CoA in the liver is converted into ketones which are transported to other tissues. In these tissues they are converted back to acetyl-CoA to enter the cancer cycle. Glucagon is produced when the blood sugar is too low and this causes the liver to start breaking the glycogen into glucose. Since diets do not eat more carbohydrates, there is no glycogen in the liver to be broken down, so the liver converts fat into free fatty acids and ketones, and this process is called ketosis. Because of this, the body is forced to use fat as a primary fuel source.

Main effects

The effects of the Atkins Diet continue to be the subject of much debate. Some studies conclude that the Atkins diet helps prevent cardiovascular disease, lowers low-density lipoprotein cholesterol, and increases the amount of HDL, or so-called "good" cholesterol. Some studies suggest that diet may contribute to osteoporosis and kidney stones. A University of Maryland study in which subjects gained increased calorie content as their weight began to decline showed higher LDL cholesterol and markers of inflammation.

Cholesterol

According to Harper in a year-long study, the concentration of high-density lipoprotein cholesterol increased, and insulin resistance improved much more in dieters following the Atkins Diet than in those following a low-fat, low-calorie diet. Harper also mentions that there had not been enough previous research to allow him to confidently say that Atkins is safe to be recommended for patients.

Methylglyoxal

A 2005 study by Beisswenger and colleagues compared levels of glycotoxin methylglyoxal before and after starting the Atkins Diet. MG is associated with blood vessels and tissue damage, and is higher in people with poorly controlled diabetes. The study found that MG levels doubled shortly after diet was started, noting that MG cause was related to the presence of ketosis. An increase in acetol and acetone was found, indicating that MG was produced by oxidation. MG also emerged as a by-product of triglyceride breakdown and from lipoxidation.

Whether increased methylglyoxal is harmful to humans has been questioned by the Indian Association for the Growth of Science, which in a 2008 critical review of various studies state, "The authors present a brief critical review of studies indicating both the toxic and beneficial effects of methylglyoxal and suggest, that the beneficial effects of methylglyoxal outweigh its toxic effects ". Although it does not draw any definitive conclusions, the Indian Association for the Growing of Science recommends further studies, especially in the field of using methylglyoxal to cure or treat cancer.

The four stages

There are four stages in the Atkins Diet: induction, ongoing weight loss, pre-maintenance, and lifetime maintenance.

Induction

Induction is the most restrictive phase of the Atkins Nutritional Approach. Two weeks is recommended for this phase. It is intended to prompt the body to quickly enter a state of ketosis. Carbohydrate intake is limited to less than 20 net grams per day; Of this amount, 12 to 15 net grams should come in the form of salad greens and other vegetables such as broccoli, spinach, pumpkin, cauliflower, mayonnaise, tomatoes and asparagus. A total of 54 vegetables are allowed by Atkins. The allowable foods include 4 to 6 ounces per meal of meat, poultry, fish, seafood, poultry or eggs; up to 4 ounces of hard or semi-solid cheese such as cheddar cheese; most salad vegetables; other low-carbohydrate vegetables; and butter, oil and vegetable oils olives. Drinking eight glasses of water a day is a requirement in this phase. Alcoholic beverages are not allowed during induction. Caffeine is allowed in moderate amounts as long as it does not cause cramp or low blood sugar. If a caffeine addiction is clear, it is best to avoid it until later stages of the diet. A daily multivitamin with minerals is also recommended. A normal amount of food on induction is about 20 grams of naturally occurring sugars from vegetables, at least 100 grams of fat, and approx. 18 ounces of protein or 150 grams.

The induction phase is usually when many see the main weight loss reports of loss of 5 to 10 pounds per week are not uncommon when Induction is combined with daily exercise. Many Atkins supporters use Ketostix, small chemically reactive strips used by diabetics, but current recommendations discourage use due to inaccurate measurements.

These let the dieter screen when entering the ketosis or fat burning phase, but are not always accurate for non-diabetic users. Other indicators of ketosis include a metallic taste in the mouth, or the sweet smell of ketones on the breath or sweat.

Continuous weight loss

The ongoing weight loss phase of Atkins consists of small, incremental increases in carbohydrate intake, but remains at a level where weight loss occurs. The goal of daily carbohydrate intake is increased weekly by 5 net grams, a very low amount of carbohydrate. One goal in this "ongoing" phase is to find the "critical carbohydrate level to lose" for the individual and to determine what foods a person can incorporate without triggering cravings. This phase of Atkins' diet lasts until the weight is within 10 pounds of the target weight.

In the first week of ongoing weight loss, Atkins Dieters is instructed to add a small serving of nuts or seeds. The next week, one should follow the "carbohydrate ladder", and add berries. The ladder has 9 steps and foods should be added in that order. One can skip a step if one does not intend to include this food group in one's permanent way of eating. The steps for legumes, high carbohydrate fruits, starchy vegetables and whole grains are not added until the maintenance phase. They are then incorporated into modest quantities.

The steps are as follows:

- Foundation vegetables
- Nuts and seeds
- Berry
- Whole milk and yogurt
- Pulses
- tomato juice

- Other fruits
- Starchy vegetables
- Whole grains

Alcohol is also allowed, but is no longer a specific step on the ladder. Low-carbohydrate drinks such as spirits and dry wines are preferred, and should of course be included in the daily carb allowance.

Pre-maintenance

Daily net carbohydrate intake is increased again, this time by 10 grams each week from the latter groupings, and the key goal in this phase is to find the "Critical Carbohydrate Level for Maintenance". This is the maximum number of carbohydrates a dieter can eat each day without gaining weight. This may well be above the level of carbohydrates that induce ketosis on a test stick. As a result, it is not necessary to maintain a positive ketosis test long term.

Dieters may be able to add some of the banned carbohydrates back into their diet once a week. In this phase, according to the Atkins Diet, one's body begins to lose the protection of ketosis as one prepares for the final phase, which is Lifetime Maintenance.

Dieters are encouraged to continue drinking at least eight glasses of water a day, and to increase their daily carbohydrate count by 10 grams each week as long as they continue to lose weight. The Atkins plan recommends that when dieters reach their goal weight and are able to maintain that level for a month or so, they can increase their daily carb consumption by another 10 grams to see if possible without gaining. If you gain weight at this level, the plan recommends reducing back levels of carbohydrates in 10 gram increments. Finding your individual turning point can take several weeks.

Lifetime maintenance

This phase is intended to carry on the habits acquired in the previous stages and avoid the common end-of-diet mindset that can return people to their past habits and past weight. Whole, unprocessed food choices are highlighted, with the option of falling back to an earlier stage if you start gaining weight.

Popularity

Atkins' nutritional approach gained widespread popularity in 2003 and 2004. At the height of its popularity, one in eleven North American adults was on a diet. This large following was blamed for large declines in carbohydrate-heavy foods such as pasta and rice: sales fell 8.2 and 4.6 percent, respectively, in 2003. Dietary success was even blamed for a decline in Krispy Kreme sales. Trying to capitalize on the "low-carb craze," many companies released special product lines that were low in carbohydrates.

In 2003 Atkins died of a fatal head injury due to a fall in ice, and while he had a history of heart disease, Ms. Atkins was quoted as stating that the circumstances surrounding his death from an epidural hematoma had nothing to do with his diet or history of viral cardiomyopathy.

July 31, 2005 Atkins nutritional company filed for Chapter 11 bankruptcy protection after the percentage of adults on diet dropped to two percent and sales of Atkins brand declined sharply in the second half of 2004. The company continues to operate and diet plan is still popular, although it has not regained its former popularity.

Scientific research

Due to considerable controversy about the Atkins Diet and even discrepancies in interpreting the results of specific studies, it is difficult to objectively summarize research in a way that reflects the scientific consensus. Although there has been some research conducted throughout the twentieth century, most directly relevant scientific studies, both those directly analyzing the Atkins Diet and those analyzing similar diets, have taken place in the 1990s and early 2000s. The ones, and as such, are relatively new. Scientists and other experts have published articles and studies that run the gamut from promoting the safety and efficacy of the diet, to questioning its long-term validity, to directly condemning it as dangerous. A major early criticism of the Atkins Diet was, that there were no studies evaluating the effect of Atkins out a few months. But studies began to emerge in the mid-to-late 2000s, assessing low carbohydrate diets over much longer periods, controlled studies, as long as two years and vision studies, as long as two decades

In addition to research into the effects of Atkins and other low-carbohydrate diets, some research has directly addressed other areas of health affected by low-carbohydrate diets. For example, contrary to popular belief that low-carbohydrate diets damage heart, a study found that women who eat low-carbohydrate, high-fat / protein diets had the same or slightly lower risk of coronary heart disease, compared to women who eat high carbohydrate, low fat diet. Other studies have found potential benefits for people with type 2 diabetes, cancer and epilepsy. A study comparing two levels of low-carbohydrate diets found that both had positive effects in terms of insulin sensitivity, weight loss, and fat loss, while the ketogenic diet showed slightly higher risk of inflammation and somewhat lower perceived levels of energy described as"

A 2007 study conducted at Stanford University Medical School, A to Z Weight Loss Study, compared the Atkins Diet with Zone, Ornish, and LEARNING diets in a randomized group of 311 overweight premenopausal women over a 12-month period. The study found that weight loss was significantly higher for the Atkins Diet compared to the

25

other three diets. Secondary factors, such as HDL-C, triglycerides and systolic blood pressure were also found to have improved to healthier levels compared to the other diets.

A 2012 study conducted at Boston Children's Hospital compared a very low carbohydrate diet with a low fat, high carbohydrate diet, and a low glycemic index diet. Reduction of dormant metabolism as a result of dieting, a key factor in diet failure, was the smallest in a very low carbohydrate diet. In addition, measured total energy consumption in patients was the highest in very low carbohydrate diets, suggesting that a very low carbohydrate diet would be the most likely to produce a sustained weight loss. One possible negative side effect was that C-reactive protein, a marker of possible future cardiovascular disease, trended somewhat higher in the very low carbohydrate diet.

In January 2004, the BBC Two science program Horizon broadcast the results of trials comparing Atkins to other diets. Dr. Joe Millward of the University of Surrey, who led research, concluded that Atkins Dieters lost weight because they ate fewer calories, just as people on low-fat diets do. The program also attributed to Atkins' weight loss that carbohydrates are the least filling foods. Professor Arne Astrup, of the Royal Veterinary & amp; In the Copenhagen Agricultural College, a study comparing one group of people on a high protein diet to another group on a high carbohydrate diet was conducted. According to Astrup, the group eating more protein lost significantly more weight because protein is easier filling, and thus members of this group consumed fewer calories, even though they had free access to whatever foods,

Controversies

An analysis conducted by Forbes magazine found that the sample menu from Atkins's nutritional approach is one of the top five in the expense category of the ten plans Forbes analyzed. This was due to the inclusion of recipes with some high-cost ingredients such as lobster tails, which were put in the book to demonstrate the range of foods that could be consumed on diet. The analysis showed that the median average of the ten diets was approx. 50% higher, and Atkins 80% higher than the US national average. The Atkins Diet was cheaper than the Jenny Craig diet and more expensive than the Weight Watchers.

Low carbohydrate diet has been the subject of heated debate in medical circles for three decades. They are still controversial and only recently have any serious research supported some aspects of Atkins' claims, especially for short-term weight loss. In a comparison study by Dansinger and colleagues, the goal was to compare popular diets such as Atkins, Ornish, Weight Watchers, and Zone for the amount of weight lost, and a heart disease risk reduction. In the study there were 160 participants and it lasted for 1 year. All subjects were obese at baseline and had an increased risk of heart disease. One of the diets was assigned to each person.

The Atkins Diet group ate 20 g CHO a day, with a gradual increase to 50 g daily. However, according to Table 2 of the study, increased to well over 130 g after the second month and up to 190 g by the sixth month. At this point, the Atkins Diet group was eating carbohydrates similar to the other three groups. Zone group ate a 40-30-30% diet of carbohydrates, fat and proteins respectively. The Weight Watchers group was keeping "points" of their food at a specific range, based on their weight. The group that was supposed to represent the Ornish diet ate a diet very unlike the Ornish diet that had been shown to reverse heart disease, taking in 30% of calories from fat instead of the suggested 10%, up to 20 grams of saturated fat a day, and only 15 grams of dietary fiber, indicating that the diet was not based on whole vegetable foods like the typical Ornish diet. The weight was taken at the beginning, blood pressure and a blood test at the beginning, after 2 months, 6 months and 12 months. All four diets resulted in modest weight loss and improvement in multiple cardiac risk factors, with no significant differences between diets.

Others in the scientific community also raise serious concerns:

Dr. Robert Eckel of the American Heart Association says that high-protein; low-carbohydrate diets put people at risk for heart disease. A long-term study published in the New England Journal of Medicine in 2006 found that while women on low-carb diets were generally healthier than those on high-carbohydrate diets, women eat more protein and fat from vegetable sources, rather than from animal sources, had a lower risk of heart disease.

A 2001 scientific review by Freedman et al. and published in peer-reviewed scientific journal Obesity Research concluded that the low-carb Dieters' initial benefit in weight loss was a result of increased water loss and that after the first period, low carbohydrate diet produces similar fat loss to other diets with similar calorie intake.

The May 2004 Annals of Internal Medicine study found that "less harmful effects" of diarrhea, general weakness, rashes and muscle cramps "were more frequent in the low-carbohydrate diet group".

Misunderstandings about diet

Many people think that the Atkins Diet promotes eating unlimited amounts of fatty meats and cheeses. This was allowed and promoted in early editions of the book. In the latest version, not written by the now deceased Dr. Atkins, this is not promoted. The Atkins Diet does not impose caloric restriction, or certain protein limits, with Atkins saying in his book that this plan is "not a license for the gorge," but promotes eating protein until saturated rather. The director of research and education for Atkins Nutritionals, Collette Heimowitz, has stated that the newer versions are intended to clarify instead replace the correct advice in the older books.

A common misconception is due to the confusion of the induction phase and the rest of the diet. The rules for the induction phase have changed since the first printing of the Atkins Diet Revolution, where all carbohydrates were counted the same. Today's version of the diet distinguishes carbohydrates, counting only "net carbs" against the daily total. The first two weeks of the Atkins Diet are strict, with only 20g of 'net' carbs allowed per day. The Net Carbs number reflects grams of carbohydrate that is said to significantly impact blood sugar, and therefore sugar alcohol carbohydrates are not counted and neither are those in fiber when you make the newer version of the Atkins plan.

Atkins says that a dieter can safely stay on the induction phase for months if the person has a lot of weight to lose. However, induction is just one step to getting the body fat; and cure cravings for high carbohydrate foods. Gradually, through stages of diet, carbohydrate levels are raised, although carbohydrates are still significantly below USDA norms. Once weight loss goals are reached, carbohydrate levels are raised again to a state of equilibrium where no weight is lost or gained, which may or may not be below USDA norms, depending on the individual's metabolism, age and their exercise level.

Dr. Eric Westman, director of Duke University's Lifestyle Medicine Clinic and co-author of The New Atkins for a New You Think Low-Carb or Atkins should be viable options among diets.

"The Atkins Diet was labeled as a high-fat diet," Westman said in an interview with The New York Times. "We've been told over the past 40 years that fat in the diet is bad. Now we know that fat is not bad. What has happened is that there is a paradigm shift in thinking about carbohydrates, fat and protein and health. "

Atkins Supplements

Atkins Nutritionals, Inc. was founded in 1989 by Atkins to promote the sale of Atkins branded products. Following his death, declining popularity of the diet and a reduction in demand for Atkins products, Atkins Nutritionals, Inc. filed for Chapter 11 bankruptcy protection on July 31, 2005 citing losses of $ 340,000,000. The company emerged from bankruptcy on January 10, 2006 to introduce "a new business strategy focusing on providing tasty portable foods with a unique nutritional benefit to healthy, active men and women." Although the marketing focus has changed, the products are still low-carb. It is also indicated on the packages the phase of Atkin's nutritional approach where they can be used.

With Atkins Diet

There are a few phases within the Atkins diet, the initial phase of which is usually the most difficult. This initial phase can have several typical side effects because you eat very few carbohydrates. These include headache, moodiness, bad breath, fatigue, bowel changes, and mental fatigue. Although the first stage of the Atkins diet can be difficult, it is certainly worth it in the long run.

- Drink coffee and tea. A typical side effect of following a low-carbohydrate diet such as the Atkins diet is that the body system is in a state of ketosis. That means that your body will get energy from ketones instead of glucose (a carbohydrate), as it normally does. Headache is one of the consequences that is the most common.

An easy and natural way to get rid of the headache is to drink something with caffeine in it. Research has shown that a little caffeine can relieve the headache.

Headache often occurs when the blood vessels in the brain expand, causing them to press against the skull. Caffeine causes the vessels to contract again so that they become thinner, reducing the pain.

Caffeine works quickly, and you usually notice relief within 30 minutes. The effect lasts for three to five hours.

Both coffee and tea are sources of caffeine, but coffee contains more caffeine. A 240 ml cup of coffee contains between 80 and 200 mg of caffeine. Drink one or two cups to relieve the headache.

Although you also find caffeine in soft drinks, sports drinks, and energy drinks, these drinks are not on the list of approved drinks within the Atkins diet.

- Try self-care products. In addition to headaches, ketosis, and a low-carbohydrate diet can also make you feel nauseous and change bowel movements. By taking self-care products, you can reduce these side effects.

If a cup of hot coffee does not help against the headache, you can take a painkiller. They are safe for most healthy people to use and provide relief from pain. Also, you can opt for a painkiller with caffeine, so that the medicine works faster and more effectively.

If you notice that you are clogged or have diarrhea, you can also take a self-care remedy to alleviate these side effects. Take a mild laxative or a fiber supplement if you cannot go to the toilet. If you are hidden too long, it will get worse, and you will need more aggressive treatment, such as an enema.

Nausea is a different side effect that can make the first days or weeks of the Atkins diet more difficult. Drink ginger tea or ginger ale, but avoid dairy products, because that can make you sicker. You can also take a self-care remedy for nausea.

- Beat peppermints and sugar-free chewing gum. Another temporary side effect of the Atkins diet is bad breath. Again, this is often due to ketosis, but you can easily remedy it.

A good way to avoid bad breath is to brush your teeth regularly. Consider bringing a travel toothbrush and a small tube of toothpaste. Brush more often than usual and also thoroughly brush the back of your tongue.

There are also mouthwashes that contain antibacterial components that can help fight bad breath.

In addition to a strict oral care regime, you can suck on mints or chew sugar-free chewing gum. Make sure you pay good attention to whether the amount of sugars fits within your diet.

- Don't do too much. It is normal for you to be a little tired or drowsy the first few days or weeks of the Atkins diet. Limit your physical exercise until these side effects are over.

Because the Atkins diet restricts you a bit, especially about the number of carbohydrates, you don't have to physically exhaust yourself.

It is recommended to do moderate to intensive cardio training for 150 minutes every week, as well as strength training for one to two days a week. This can be a bit too much at the start of your diet. Instead of doing moderate to intensive cardio training, you can try to do the same amount of not too intensive cardio. Activities such as walking or quiet cycling may be easier and more fun if you stick to a strict diet.

Exercise can also provide a positive mentality if your diet is difficult to sustain.

- Go to bed earlier. It is not surprising that you are a little tired or even grumpy during the first days of the Atkins diet. Make sure you sleep enough to counteract these effects.

You need seven to nine hours of sleep every night. If you don't touch it now, you will find that you get really tired and drowsy if you eat little carbohydrates.

Try to go to bed a little quicker each day during the first phase of the Atkins diet. Stay a little longer if you can.

- Set up a support group. It can be useful to have a support group with every diet so that you can encourage each other and keep up better.

Many studies show that people who are supported by friends or family maintain a diet better and lose more weight than people without a support group.

Tell your friends or family that you are going to follow the Atkins diet and say how much you want to lose weight. Ask if they want to support you and if they might want to join you.

Also, you will find all sorts of options for seeking support on the Atkins diet website. Take a look at their website for more information.

- Seek support. There will be challenges with every diet. If you have a group of people that you support, you will get more motivation and encouragement to stick to your new diet.

Ask friends, families, and colleagues to support you. Tell them about your new diet and your long-term goals. Maybe they even want to participate.

A support group can also assist you with the mental difficulties of following a diet. It can be a challenge to maintain a strict diet such as the Atkins diet day in, day out.

Research has revealed that people who have a support group maintain a diet longer, stick to it better, and lose more weight than people who don't.

- Start a diary. Keeping a diary about your new diet and long-term goals can be a good way to deal with the difficulties associated with following such a diet. Sometimes writing in a diary alone is enough to keep you on the right track.

Use a pen and notebook or an online app to start a diary. You don't have to write every day, but it helps to put your thoughts on paper.

You can also use your diary to keep track of your progress.

. Start with the Atkins diet

- View which foods and recipes are allowed. When you start a new diet, you first have to understand what it means, and what you can and cannot eat. Then the transition to the diet is a lot easier.

The Atkins diet is a very particular type of low-carbohydrate diet. It is divided into four phases with a separate list of foods and portion sizes that are allowed within each phase.

In phase 1 you are allowed to eat full-fat cheese, fats, and oil, fish and shellfish, poultry, eggs, meat, herbs, vegetables that do not contain starch and green leafy vegetables (the so-called basic vegetables).

Stock up on these foods so that you have everything that is permitted within reach to prepare meals and snacks.

- Eat every two to three hours. Eating every few hours will prevent you from getting hungry, but it is especially advisable during the first phase of the Atkins diet.

With this diet, it is recommended to eat three meals plus two snacks a day or to eat five to six small meals a day. Make sure you never wait longer than three hours to eat.

If you sit between meals or snacks for more than three hours, you get too hungry and are more likely to eat something that is not allowed because you are starving.

Always take a meal or snack with you when you go out. Then you avoid eating something that is not on the allowed list when you get hungry.

- Eat the right amount of carbohydrates. You will notice that during each phase of the Atkins diet, a very specific amount of carbohydrates per day is recommended. It is important to follow this guideline very carefully.

During the first phase of the diet, you are allowed 20 grams of carbohydrates per day. It is expedient not to exceed that amount, but also to ensure that you eat at least 18 grams of carbohydrates.

If you eat less than 18 grams of carbohydrates, you do not lose weight earlier, but you probably do not eat enough basic vegetables.

Spread the 20 grams of carbohydrates throughout the day. This makes you feel more even throughout the day. If you take all 20 grams of carbohydrates for breakfast, you will experience more side effects in the afternoon.

- Drink enough. With the Atkins diet, as with most other diets, it is recommended to drink a lot.

Water is essential for your overall health, even if you are not on a diet. Also, drinking enough, as previously mentioned, can prevent nausea and blockage.

The Atkins diet suggests drinking at least eight large glasses of water a day. General guidelines even suggest that you should drink 13 glasses of water a day. This depends on your age, gender, and level of activity.

You should not be thirsty all day, and your urine should be clear at the end of the day if you have drunk enough.

- Consider taking supplements. The Atkins diet recommends that you maintain Phase 1 for at least two weeks or until you are 5 - 7 pounds away from your goal weight. If you want to lose a lot of weight, you may have to take dietary supplements.

The initial stage of the Atkins diet does extremely limited and removes various food groups (such as fruit, starchy vegetables, and grains) from your diet. If you plan to maintain this phase for a longer period, it is a good idea to take dietary supplements to prevent you from getting a shortage of certain nutrients.

A multivitamin is a good "backup." Take one a day to ensure that you get all the necessary nutrients every day.

You can also consider taking 500-1000 mg of calcium per day because you do not eat dairy.

About the Atkins Cure

It is astonishing that the Atkins cure is still one of the most popular diet. Nowadays you can find it under the name LCHF (low carb high fat), keto or ketogenic diet. I mean, if a 'cure' lasts so long, it must mean that it has some benefits and some decisive results.

Let's take a closer look at what all the fuss is about.

What is the Atkins cure?

The website states that the Atkins cure: "limits carbohydrates (sugars) so the body burns fat, including body fat, as fuel". They even display this informative little image to help you understand this definition.

Here's the idea behind Atkins: fill the body in a way that maintains a renewable energy level instead of a fluctuating sugar level, which is exacerbated by a large intake of carbohydrates. In this course, you consume a few carbohydrates, a moderate amount of protein and a lot of fat.

Here is a list of foods recommended by the Atkins Cure:

- Vegetables with many dietary fiber
- protein
- Healthy fats
- dairy products
- Low glycemic fruits

When following the Atkins course, avoid the following foods:

- Sugar
- Refined flour
- trans fats

But it turns out that Atkins is more intricate than that. The cure actually has 4 stages.

Atkins Diet Phase Two And Sustained Weight Loss

The second phase is continuous weight loss (OWL). It begins after two weeks on the strictly low carbohydrate induction phase geared to jumping on your weight loss.

In the OWL phase, carbohydrates are slowly and carefully added to the diet. Your weight loss lowers to a recommended one to two pounds a week. Dieters in this phase experiment to find out how much carbohydrate they can eat and still lose weight. This point is called their critical carbohydrate level for losing (CCLL).

Starts Atkins in phase two

You do not need to start the Atkins diet during the strict induction phase. For some people, it is more appropriate to start in the OWL phase. These include those who have a weight loss goal of 14 pounds or less, vegetarians, those who want more food, and those who don't mind losing weight slowly in the first two weeks.

Phase length

The OWL phase continues until you are five to 10 pounds from your target weight. At that point, you will enter the third phase, Prevalence.

Objectives of the OWL phase

Determining the Critical Carbohydrate Level to Lose (CCLL)

To expand food choices and learn how to make smart

To continue weight loss at a safe rate

Continuing to eat on a carb level low enough to limit cravings and appetites

What you eat

Every week during OWL, you increase your daily carb supplement by 5 grams until the proper level is reached, no more than 40 grams per day. As more carbohydrate gradually gets to the feed during this phase, Atkins recommends it be done in a priority order, he calls the "Carbohydrate Ladder", where more vegetables are the first foods to be added and whole grains are the last.

Atkins provides lists of foods at 5 gram intervals to help dieters figure out their daily menus. You can now start adding nuts, seeds, berries and some cheeses to your diet and you will eat natural fats. You can also purchase the commercially made Atkins foods to use as convenient foods in your diet.

To support good nutrition, you will continue to take a multivitamin, mineral and omega-3 supplement. It is also important to be well hydrated with eight glasses of water or other permitted drinks a day.

Menus

Your menus will depend on your carb level. First, you just want to add 5 carb grams of vegetables to your day. Then you can have some berries with breakfast or as dessert. As your diet expands, you add food from the ladder. The book "Atkins for Life" has examples of menus at various carb levels.

In this phase, it is important to carefully track your carbs. Atkins offers an online carb counter, diet tracker and journal as well as a mobile app to count carbs and track your diet.

Pre-treatment in Atkins diet phase three

As dieters near their goal, weight loss declines even more, with more carbohydrate added to the diet. Individuals figure out how much carbohydrate each can safely eat without gaining weight. This point is called the Atkins Carbohydrate Equilibrium (ACE).

How it works

Phase three is a time to tinker with the diet, to find out what foods can be trigger foods, what the reactions are for different types of foods, and determining how much carbohydrate is too much, leading to cravings, weight gain and other unwanted symptoms.

It is interesting how different people react to different foods. For example, some may do well with legumes while fruit brings cravings. Therefore, it is very important at this stage to walk slowly and observe carefully.

What to eat

Carbohydrate is added, according to Atkins Carbohydrate Ladder introduced in phase two. 10 grams of carb can be added per day, or a larger (20-30 grams) "treat" can be added two or three times a week.

Examples of foods to be added during Pre-processing:

Assuming that in Phase 2 you added foods from the "Nuts and Seeds" and "Berries and Melons" rings in the Atkins ladder, you can either add more of these foods or move on to the next steps:

- Legumes: Add 1/3 cup legumes such as lentils, black beans or chickpeas
- Other fruits: like a medium peach or plum , half a medium apple or a medium kiwi fruit
- Starchy Vegetables: Like half a medium sweet potato, 1/3 cup can, or 3/4 cup slices.
- Whole Grains: Half a cup of most grains is up about 20 grams of net carb, so you will go very easily on them. Consider making a salad with 1/4 cup of cooked quinoa or brown rice poured in. Or if you want some hot cereal, 3 tablespoons of oat bran will cook up to half a cup and is approx. 10 grams net carb.

Phase Length

The weight should deliberately drop slowly - Atkins recommends a 2-3 month period to lose the last 10 pounds or so. Many people find that they lose even slower - about a pound a month - in this phase.

1) To find out the amount of carbohydrate that can be eaten without gaining weight. (Atkins Carbohydrate Equilibrium - ACE)

2) To slowly lose weight to the goal.

3) Learning to maintain weight by using the Atkins approach.

Menus

Menus, of course, depend on the amount and types of food eaten in a given week. There are sample menus at various carbohydrate levels in Atkins for Life and The New Atkins for a New You.

Cardiovascular disease and type 2 diabetes on the Atkins course

Thanks to the low-carb lifestyle that Atkins promotes, this cure is also a bonus to the cardiovascular system.

According to a study by Harvard TH Chan School of Public Health, it found that:

Women who ate a low-carbohydrate diet with a high fat or protein content had a 30% lower risk of heart disease and a 20% lower risk of type 2 diabetes compared to women who ate a low-carbohydrate, low-fat diet.

However, it is important to note that the study added that "women who ate low carbohydrate diets who had a high content of animal fat or proteins did not have the same benefits".

Another study concluded that replacing carbohydrates with protein or even healthy monounsaturated fats helps lower blood pressure, improve lipid levels, lower your overall risk of cardiovascular disease and lose weight. It sounds like Atkins in a nutshell.

Now that we have pointed out some of the benefits, what about the potential risk factors associated with the Atkins cure?

What are the potential dangers of the Atkins cure?

Without carbohydrates, you will begin to lack essential dietary fiber that will keep your digestion going.

In your effort to cut the "bad" away, you may be omitting important nutrients that come only from a varied diet.

Remember, you should always talk to your doctor before starting a new cure. Just because you know someone who has lost a lot of weight on a particular diet doesn't mean it works for everyone.

During the research of the Atkins cure, there was an updated spin-off of the original: the Eco-Atkins cure.

Eco-Atkins diet

The Eco-Atkins Cure is a low-carb, protein-rich version of the Atkins Cure for vegetarians and vegans. That is, the proteins come from the plant kingdom, such as nut butter and chia seeds.

In one study, participants were divided into the following groups and monitored for one month:

- A vegan diet that excludes both animal products and by-products, such as eggs. (Eco-Atkins Group).
- A lacto-vegetarian diet which includes dairy products such as milk, cheese, yogurt, etc.

Participants in both categories were overweight. Although both groups lost weight due to the limited caloric intake, the Eco-Atkins group had a greater decrease in their LDL cholesterol compared to the lacto-vegetarian group.

This cure is also subject to all the disadvantages of other vegan cures.

Ketosis: What was that exactly again?

Short Digression: The preferred energy of your body is carbohydrates. The carbs are broken down into specific sugar molecules, glucose, and are released into the blood. The blood sugar level rises and your pancreas produces the so-called memory hormone insulin. It ensures that the energy in the form of sugar is transported into the cells. In particular, your brain relies on carbs. The downside: if your muscle cells and your brain do not consume the energy completely, it will be stored very quickly as an extra cushion in the fat cells.

Here is the ketosis help: By your body's favorite source of energy carbohydrates take away, he must look for an alternative source of energy and what is more obvious than to choose fat? Of that, you provide him on the fat-based diet much available and also have your body own large stores on the stomach, hips, and buttocks. For energy to be produced from fats, the body has developed a contingency plan called ketosis. Your body produces so-called ketone bodies in the liver from the free fatty acids of your fat cells; this is a water-soluble glucose alternative that is well transported in the blood and can cross the blood-brain barrier so that your brain gets the much-needed energy. In ketosis, you draw your energy from fats and not from the body's protein, the muscles. The ketogenic diet, therefore, promises fat loss without muscle loss! By the way: ketone bodies should provide about 25% more energy than glucose and also much more even.

The ketosis begins as soon as your insulin level falls below a certain value. When this value is reached varies from person to person, but there is the possibility of finding out about blood, urine, or breath tests. However, whether you are in ketosis, you also notice physical symptoms such as increased urination, dry mouth, great thirst, less hunger, bad breath, strange taste in the mouth and increased concentration and energy.

Likewise, when ketosis ceases, dry eyes, bad sleep, (hot) hunger, and a sudden, heavy increase in weight are possible signs.

Ketosis is also reached if you do not eat for a long time. Therefore it is also called "hunger metabolism" and seen as an imitation of fasting metabolism. When your body is in ketosis for long periods, keto-adaptation is used: your body has switched its primary source of energy from carbs to fats. While this is not completely the case with the Atkins diet, with a completely ketogenic diet a three-month ketosis phase is being discussed, but your body is still learning to use the fats as an energy source. Later in the Atkins diet, the carbs gradually become smaller in moderation to the extent that will not let you increase again. The ketosis is then stopped again; it is used in the diet so only for losing weight.

How is the Atkin's diet different from the ketogenic diet?

It can be easy to get confused with these two diet plans because both focus on the consumption of low carbohydrates. However, there are still a few distinctions about each of them.

Ketogenic diets are based on the principles of eating a specific amount or a percentage of the macronutrients in your daily diet. It enables you to eat a lot of fat up to 60%, an adequate amount of protein around 35 %, while only encouraging very low carbohydrate consumption by only 5 %. This helps force the body to ketosis, where it uses "ketones" as an When there are not enough carbohydrates in the body for a prolonged period, the body through the liver enters our fat deposits and begins to convert fats into fatty acids and ketones that it uses as energy. This process helps the body lose a large amount of fat when it is in ketosis.

The Atkins diet also gives a promising result when it comes to losing weight, but it allows you to eat as much fat and protein as you want since you only consume a small number of carbohydrates.

The diet is a product of Dr. Robert Coleman Atkins, an American doctor, and cardiologist, and is a diet that involves starting with ketosis and staying in ketosis until you have lost a considerable amount of weight. This is called the "induction" phase of the diet. After induction, gradually reintroduce carbohydrates, making sure they are still low in carbohydrates and avoid carbohydrates and unwanted processed sugars. And that is one of the main differences between Ketosis and Atkins.

Ketosis is a very effective way to lose weight since it is the metabolism of starvation. Your body stops trying to burn sugars as fuel and begins to burn your fat reserves.

Few differences between them:

- Ketogenic is 60% fat, while Atkins allows unlimited fat consumption
- Ketogenic allows 35% protein while Atkins allows unlimited protein consumption
- Ketogenic allows 5% carbohydrates, while Atkins allows just under 50g of carbohydrates
- Atkins is more comfortable to follow than the ketogenic diet and a short-term weight loss diet, but it also comes with different health risks
- The ketogenic diet is a more precise way of eating to change your metabolism
- The ketogenic diet offers much better long-term health benefits once you get used to implementing it in your life.

Related of "How is the Atkin's diet different from the ketogenic diet?"

The ketogenic diet is VERY specific about the proportion of macronutrients and is in a state of ketosis (hence the name of the diet). While Atkins is not like that, it is a low carb diet with different "carbohydrate allocation phases."

Ketogenic diet Fat / Protein / Carbohydrate: 75% + / 15-20% / 5-10%

Atkins is not so strict with macros. It is more a low carb diet, when you specifically restrict the number of carbohydrates, not necessarily tracking the intake of fats and proteins as much.

Atkins especially modified and new, although it is also about putting your body in a metabolic state in which you burn fat as your main source of fuel.

At the moment Atkins and Keto make a kind of mixture with all the modified versions, keto and Atkins cycling, etc.

Having said that, from memory the key distinction to remember is that, while a ketogenic diet is low in carbohydrates (and that is why at least below 50 g / day, for some even less), modest protein (limited to avoid too much excess protein that can result in gluconeogenesis, resulting in increased blood sugar and insulin, etc.) and high fat content, the Atkins diet is high in fat, high in protein and low in in carbohydrates.

Also, the truly low carbohydrate period in Atkins lasts only the first 2 weeks, after which it begins to add more starchy vegetables to your diet slowly. In a ketogenic diet, you continue to maintain your carbohydrate intake generally low essentially undefined, although, of course, you can cycle from time to time or allow yourself more freedom than at the beginning concerning carbohydrates (which is fine if has been adapted, etc. of course)

Therefore, to clarify, a ketogenic diet keeps you in nutritional ketosis, regardless of your intake of carbohydrates and proteins, but begins as low in carbohydrates, high in fat and moderate in protein.

Diet of Ketonic vs. Atkins

The Atkins diet is a low carb diet, but the difference is in the number of proteins and carbohydrates that you can ingest per day.

The Atkins diet is based mainly on proteins, while the ketogenic diet suggests an average protein intake.

Main differences

- Ketogenic suggest about 65% fat, while Atkins allows unlimited fat consumption
- Keto allows up to 40% protein, while Atkins allows unlimited protein consumption
- Ketogenic allows 5% carbohydrates - Atkins allows 50 g of carbohydrates

Atkins is more comfortable to follow than the ketogenic diet, but it also presents different health risks. The keto diet gives much better long-term health benefits.

Phase 1 of Atkins is a ketogenic diet.

The next 3 phases will gradually reintroduce carbohydrates into your diet.

List of healthy foods of carbohydrates and dietary foods

Paleo and ketogenic diets are similar, even Atkins is similar if you look at their principles? Yes, there are slight differences that are important because they achieve very different objectives.

The Atkins diet is based mainly on proteins, that is, eating as much protein as you want and without sugars.

Ketogenic is: eat 25 g or less of carbohydrates per day, adequate amounts of protein per day, usually around 1 g per kg of body weight, and the amount of fat you want.

Simple

Atkins says to eat all the protein you want. Modern ketogenic diets emphasize fats and recommend only moderate amounts of protein.

Atkins is low in carbohydrates, but Keto has less than 25 grams of net carbohydrates and uses a more fat-rich approach.

Sample menu for the Atkins course

Phase 1 usually lasts 2 weeks, with Phase 4 being a lengthy one. Coffee and tea should be decaffeinated, but may be consumed with milk and cream.

Phase 1

Day 1

Breakfast

- 120-180 grams of smoked salmon wrapped around
- 2 tbsp. cream cheese
- 75 grams of cucumber salad

Snack / snack

- 2 celery stalks
- 2 tablespoons dressing

Breakfast chicken salad

- 120-180 grams of grilled curry
- 300 grams of mixed salad
- ½ sliced avocado
- 10 black olives
- ½ dl of alfalfa sprouts
- 2 tbsp. Italian dressing

Snack / snack

- 1 protein bar

Dinner turkey or ham salad

- 300 grams of lettuce
- 120-180 grams of turkey or ham
- 1 small tomato
- 2 tbsp. chopped onions
- 22 grams of grated cheddar cheese
- 2 tbsp. French dressing

Day 2

Breakfast scrambled eggs

- 3 eggs
- 4-6 pieces of bacon

Breakfast chicken salad

- 180 grams of grilled chicken
- 160 grams of lettuce leaves
- 1 tbsp. grated cheese
- 2 tbsp. dressing
- 1 hard boiled egg in slices

Dinner breaded fish fillet

- 200 grams of fish fillet turned into egg and grater. Fry in oil.
- 75 grams of lettuce
- 1 tomato In slices
- 1 red onion In slices
- 200 grams of broccoll cooked and turned into butter

Day 3

Breakfast

- 90 grams of cream cheese mixed with:
- 1 egg
- ¼ teaspoon of vanilla
- 1 pinch of cinnamon
- 1 tbsp. linseed

Breakfast tuna salad

- 1 can of tuna
- 4 chopped pickled cucumbers
- 1 tbsp. lemon juice
- Salt
- Pepper
- 120 grams of cheese
- 75 grams of lettuce
- Pork loin on top as much as you want now
- 1 tbsp. Salat dressing
- 1 cup salad greens

Dinner

- 180 grams of minced beef or Italian sausage
- 1 tbsp. onion powder
- 2 tbsp. crushed garlic
- 1 beef broth
- 1 tbsp. soy
- 1 can of tomato puree
- 1 DL. Water
- 2 tbsp. basil
- 2 tbsp. oregano

(Brown the meat, add everything else and simmer for 10 min.)

Serve on top:

190 grams squash in slices

Sprinkle with:

2 tbsp. parmesan or Romano cheese

150 grams of salad with 2 tbsp. dressing

Day 4

Breakfast

- 3 soft or hard boiled eggs minced and mixed with:
- 1 tbsp. freshly chopped herbs of your choice
- 1 tbsp. butter
- 1 tbsp. cream
- 4 turkey sausages

Lunch

- 200 grams of turkey or ham in strips
- 1 hard-boiled egg chopped
- 2 tbsp. grated cheese
- 150 grams of lettuce
- 2 tbsp. dressing

Dinner lamb fried in mint and rosemary twigs

- 200 grams of lamb
- 2 tbsp. freshly minted mint
- 4 rosemary twigs
- 75 grams of lettuce
- 1 tbsp. dressing

- 150 grams of cauliflower turned into butter or cream

Day 5

Breakfast omelet

- 3 eggs
- ¼ dl of cream
- 2 tbsp. spinach
- 2 tbsp. feta
- 3 tbsp. pasta sauce
- 100 grams of ham in cubes

Lunch

- 200 grams of grilled beef in strips
- 75 grams of lettuce
- 1 red onion in slices
- 1 tomato in slices
- 2 tbsp. dressing

Dinner Taco Salad

- 200 grams of minced beef (browned with taco seasoning)
- 150 grams of lettuce
- 1 chopped tomato
- 1 chopped onion
- ¼ avocado, sliced
- 5 black olives in slices
- 1 tbsp. sour cream
- 1 tbsp. grated cheese
- 2 tbsp. sugar-free taco sauce

Phase 4

Breakfast

- ½ white grapefruit
- 2 scrambled eggs with:
- 1 onion
- 2 tbsp. grated cheddar cheese

Snack / snack

- 1 protein bar
- 90 grams of blackberries

Breakfast chicken salad

- 180 grams of grilled chicken
- 150 grams of lettuce
- 90 grams of corn
- 90 grams of red pepper
- 45 grams of black beans
- 2 tbsp. dressing

Snack / snack

- 1 medium-sized carrot
- 60 grams of walnuts

Dinner

- 180 grams of steak
- 4-6 ounce flank steak
- 75 grams of mushroom sauce
- ½ cup potato mash
- 150 grams of lettuce
- 30 grams of cheese
- 75 grams of peas
- ½ dl pickled beets
- 2 tbsp. dressing

How individual is the Atkins diet?

- For all dieters, the same rules and quantities apply. So you are not individually tailored to the individual.
- Due to the high protein content of animal products, this form of diet is not adaptable to special eating habits such as vegetarianism or veganism.

How flexible is the Atkins diet?

- There is no annoying calorie counting needed, and it must be dispensed quasi only on carbohydrates. Thus, this diet is also feasible for, e.g., working people.
- No special food is needed, and a restaurant visit is no obstacle. One should do without carbohydrate-rich side dishes.

How suitable is the Atkins diet for everyday use?

- The complete abandonment of carbohydrates makes the diet quite one-sided
- Even eating out can be a problem from time to time. On the other hand, one has free choice among the allowed recipes and is not limited in the amount

How scientific is the Atkins diet?

- The success of the Atkins diet is detectable, but this is mainly due to the calorie reduction itself and not to the renunciation of carbohydrates.
- The drastic renouncement of carbohydrates is to be regardod critically since carbohydrates are the number one energy supplier for the body. So when you completely erase them from the diet, the body is forced to draw energy from muscle mass and fat. This also suffers the muscles underneath, and it can lead to muscle cramps.
- The high protein content in the diet is bad for the body in the long term. Not only does the insulin level increase, but a portion of uric acid accumulates during the division and digestion of proteins. If the protein intake is too high, the toxic substance can be deposited in the kidney and cause lasting damage. A long-term consequence can even be cardiovascular disease.

How Sustainable Is The Atkins Diet, And What Are Its Risks?

- Keeping strictly to the rules and rules of the diet, you can achieve quick results, especially in the early stages. The later stages then serve to acclimatize and adapt, so that the weight can be kept.
- However, this type of diet can / should not be maintained permanently because, due to the high proportion of animal fats, health risks are not ruled out and fatigue and impairment of the immune system can occur in the long term due to the high carbohydrate deficiency.
- The weight reduction happens very fast and not necessarily sustainable, which is why the risk of succumbing to the yo-yo effect after ending the diet is quite high.
- The principle of the Atkins diet relies on ketosis: In the absence of carbohydrates for energy metabolism, fatty acids in the liver are converted into ketone bodies to ensure energy readiness.
- However, this also carries the risk of increased triglyceride levels. Highly obese people, as well as diabetics or people who suffer from a lipid metabolism disease, usually already suffer from an increased triglyceride value anyway. The consequence of this is an increased risk of thrombosis.
- Also, the often mentioned extreme carbohydrate deficiency could lead to any amount of deficiency symptoms. Symptoms of this include fatigue, muscle cramps, high cholesterol, and lipid levels, kidney and liver damage, or even high blood pressure.

Method

To achieve effective customer success with the Atkins diet, the diet seeker should follow the four-step model: At the beginning of the phases, the goal is to limit the consumption of carbohydrates. During the subsequent phases, the declining person is slowly brought back to the consumption of carbohydrates. In the first phase of the Atkins diet, also known as the "induction phase," no more than 20 grams of carbohydrates should be ingested daily for two weeks. To calculate the exact amount of carbohydrates, calculators, and scales can be used.

Furthermore, there are numerous carbohydrate tables, from which the values can be easily read. All other foods, however, are allowed without limitation. The subsequent reduction phase already allows more carbohydrates. In the beginning week of the second phase, the carbohydrate amount is increased by five grams. This will be continued week after week until further weight reduction takes place. During this phase, the critical amount of carbohydrate is approached. The critical amount of carbohydrates is the number of carbohydrates that you continue to lose weight with. If one realizes that no weight reduction takes place, the daily amount of carbohydrates should be screwed down again. Since the Atkins diet does not include a balanced diet, dietary supplements should be used during the second phase to avoid possible deficiency symptoms.

The third phase of the diet plan should be started before reaching the target weight. It can be seen as a preparatory phase for the fourth and final phase. During this time, the daily amount of carbohydrates is increased to ten grams per week. The losers should be aware that now only a slow weight loss. If the weight reduction stops, you should go back to phase two. If the desired weight is reached, you finally reached phase four.

The fourth phase is considered to be a lifelong diet. With it, the achieved weight should be kept. It should be lived permanently according to the Atkins diet plan, which means a lot of fat and protein, little fruits and vegetables are consumed. It is important that the number of carbohydrates can always be increased until you discover more kilos on the scales again. During this time, the daily amount of carbohydrates is increased to ten grams per week. The losers should be aware that now only a slow weight loss. If the weight reduction stops, you should go back to phase two. If the desired weight is reached, you finally reached phase four.

Implementation in everyday life

The Atkins diet brings at first glance, no renunciation, only on the number of carbohydrates, should be respected. People who like to eat bread, pasta, or rice and can hardly give it up should rather choose a different diet. Even for fruit and vegetable lovers, the Atkins diet plan could be a challenge. Since no annoying calorie counting is needed, the diet can also be easily implemented for working people. However, if you plan to go on a diet with your entire family, you should choose a different diet. Especially for children who are still growing, the diet is not recommended. Because the recipes of the Atkins diet use conventional foods and do not require any extraordinary spices, can be easily bought in the familiar supermarket. Many delivery companies and restaurants are also happy to respond to the needs of their customers and leave on demand carbohydrate-side supplements easily or exchange them with others. Thus, eating out during the Atkins diet is no problem. To avoid deficiencies during diet as already mentioned dietary supplements are recommended. However, a little more money for the preparations must be included. To avoid deficiencies during diet as already mentioned dietary supplements are recommended. However, a little more money for the preparations must be included. To avoid deficiencies during diet as already mentioned dietary supplements are recommended. However, a little more money for the preparations must be included.

Scientific

Although studies prove the success of Dr. Diet's diet, Atkins, however, this is mainly due to the reduction in calorie intake. The small number of carbohydrates should be viewed critically: the brain and muscles need this nutrient. If it is supplied to the body so only slightly, it can quickly lead to unpleasant muscle spasms. The high proportion of animal fat and protein is also to be viewed critically. The cholesterol in the body can thereby be increased, which in turn can result in increased blood fat and uric acid levels. If these values are too high, the diminishing risk of developing gout or cardiovascular diseases is at risk. Atkins relies on the process of ketosis: lack of carbohydrates for energy metabolism, fatty acids In the liver are converted into ketone bodies, to ensure energy readiness. However, too much ketone formation can lead, among other things, to renal insufficiency, liver damage, constipation, hypertension, and gout, as the ketone bodies cannot be sufficiently excreted. The special diet of the Atkins diet can also increase triglyooride levels. Having too high triglyceride levels in the blood increases the risk of developing atherosclerosis and thrombosis.

In most cases, people who are overweight have diabetes or dyslipidemia already have an elevated triglyceride level anyway. Also, as the body is constantly exposed to a high intake of protein during the Atkins diet, this could put a strain on the kidneys.

Consideration of Sports

To achieve optimal weight loss, the Atkins Diet Diet Plan also includes a regular exercise program. Endurance sports such as jogging, swimming, or cycling should be run two or three times a week. Heavily overweight people should go swimming rather than jogging to protect the joints. Also, strength training is also provided. Here, too, should seriously overweight or athletic inexperienced in advance prefer to seek advice to avoid consequential damage.

Long-term effect

If you stick to the strict rules and regulations during the Atkins phases, you can expect enormous weight loss. According to the diet finder, you can already lose up to seven kilograms of weight in the first two weeks. In phase one, two and three can tumble between 0.5 to 1.5 kilograms per week. In phase four, the weight achieved is only kept. Although this phase should be regarded as a lifelong diet, it is rather discouraged due to the high proportion of animal fats and the associated health risks and consequential damages.

What differentiates LCHF from Atkins?

LCHF and Atkins are similar. Both largely refrain from carbohydrates as an energy source and are suitable for weight loss or the basic diet.

The Atkins diet is often linked to pure consumption of meat and fat. That is not right. Because only in the entry phase, the four-stage Atkins diet contains a lot of protein and fat, in the other diet phases, however, increasingly more carbohydrates from vegetables, berries, fruits and (whole grain) cereals.

LCHF sees the person

LCHF or Low Carb High Fat is less dogmatic and sees every person individually. Each body reacts differently to the intake of carbohydrates, and the health conditions play a significant role in the acceptance of carbohydrates. So there are LCHFler who consume only 5 grams of carbs daily, but others 30-50 grams and more.

Instead of carbohydrates, however, all natural fats (saturated fatty acids) occur, which should preferably be of animal origin. However, protein or protein should meet LCHF's requirements and should not be consumed excessively.

However, one principle distinguishes LCHF significantly from the Atkins diet

LCHF attaches great importance to a natural and good diet. This means that no industrially processed foods are on the menu, as well as poorly produced foods. This is especially true for animal products. Ecologically and regionally produced goods should always be given preference, if possible.

Meanwhile, the original idea of the Atkins diet has developed into a huge business that offers dietary supplements, protein shakes and bars, just to name a few products that would never be present in a classic LCHF diet.

Atkins diet pros and cons

Evaluate the Atkins Diet Negatives and Positives before you start

The Atkins diet plan has undergone many changes over the years. The strict eating plan has many unique factors that you should consider before trying to follow it. Atkins offers several benefits that can make it the perfect diet for some. But the drawbacks can rule it out for others. If you are considering using this diet to lose weight, be sure to evaluate all of Atkin's pros and cons before starting the diet.

Atkins Diet Pros

The Atkins diet works for people who prefer a structured eating plan. Here are some reasons Atkins can work for you:

- Hearty eating plan. Some people like that you can eat more food on the Atkins diet plan. For example, many men prefer this diet because the nearby foods like steaks and burgers can stay on your menu.
- Learn how to eat healthy carbs. The Atkins diet eliminates refined carbohydrates such as baked goods such as cake and white bread and encourages your intake of healthy carbohydrates, especially in the later stages of the plan. So you learn the difference between good carbs and bad carbs.
- No calorie intake. Hate to count calories then this is the diet for you. You count net carbs to lose weight, but you don't have to worry about calories. Additionally, while following this plan, you can find your ideal carbohydrate intake level.
- Significant weight loss. Many people have lost much of this plan. Some Atkins dieters lose 80 pounds or more on the plan. During

the earliest phase of the diet, called induction, rapid weight loss is common. This early weight loss can provide a boost of confidence and motivation.

- Improved health. Despite the diet's higher fat content, some Atkins dieters see improvements in their cholesterol levels. In addition, you are likely to reduce your sugar intake on this plan, which can lead to improvements in your health.
- Produced foods available. If you don't like preparing your own food all the time, Atkins snack bars and other food replacements are conveniently available in many markets and discount stores.
- Atkins resources are widely available. You'll find most of what you need to follow Atkins' plan online. Food lists and other guides can be found on their website. You will also find Atkins books and guides in bookstores and online.

Atkins Diet Cons

While some dieters enjoy the benefits of diet, others struggle to stick to Atkins' strict eating plan. These drawbacks can work against you if you start the Atkins diet.

- Reduced energy. The diet does not provide much energy in the form of carbohydrate. In fact, if you are a typical American eater before you start the diet, you will significantly reduce your carbs intake. For many dieters, this causes fatigue.
- Reduced fruit and grain intake. If you are a dieter who loves fruit, you can fight for the Atkins plan. Eventually, you can add fruits and grains to your diet , but in the early stages of the diet, your intake is limited.
- Too tight for many dieters. Low-carb diets such as Atkins can be difficult to follow because they require you to make too many

changes from the start. These dieters can enjoy an eating plan that starts with small changes.

- Separation from ordinary foods. Making low carb on the Atkins plan involves avoiding many common and popular foods, such as chips, bread and pasta. You are likely to be surrounded by these foods during induction and this may make the plan harder to follow.
- Possible mad binges. Some diets come back when they are too strict. In some cases, the restriction leads to mad binges, guilt and weight gain.
- Discomfort. There are some Atkins dieters who have experienced constipation, halitosis and sometimes dehydration as a result of dietary changes in their eating plan.
- Counting net carbohydrates can be tedious. You don't count calories, but for some dieters, counting net carbs is just as complicated and tedious, especially when eating out.
- Possible weight regains. Those who return to eating carbs usually regain all the weight they lost over the diet, and maybe even more.

The Atkins diet works for many dieters. But not for everyone. These Atkins diet pros and cons should help you decide if the plan is right for you. Compare that to other popular diet plans, such as Jenny Craig, Weight Watchers, The South Beach Diet and Nutrisystem to see how different plans can work in your life. But remember that you do not have to pay for a plan to lose weight. You can cut portion size or count calories on your own to slim down. If you are not sure of the best plan for you, talk to a registered dietitian or your doctor for guidance

.

Counting carbs

Knowing how much carbohydrate you eat is essential to a low-carb diet. One way to do this is to count carb grams.

Depending on your diet plan, you need to know whether to count total carbohydrate or net carbohydrate. For example, the way most diabetics teach carb count, total carb grams have been used, while the Atkins diet uses net carbs. Depths below approx. As a rule, 50-60 grams of carb per day consumes net carbohydrates, while diets with more carbs (up to about 200 grams of carb per day are considered "low carb" by some definitions) use the total carbs in their count.

1 - Total Carbohydrate or Net Carbs?

If you eat these foods on a low-carb diet, it is important to know how much carb they have. Adam Gault / OJO Images / Getty Images

Choosing the right type of carb count can make a difference in terms of the success of your diet plan, so be aware of this.

What is total carbohydrate? A total carb count will contain all the carbohydrate in the food, regardless of the source.

What is a Net Carb Count? When counting net carb, the fiber is subtracted from the rest of the carbohydrate. Some processed low-carbon or sugar-free foods pull out sugar alcohols and other ingredients, but be careful about this.

2 - Measurement is the most important thing!

It may sound obvious, but you can't tell how much things are in one thing if you don't know how much of it you have! It is very common for people to think that they know how much a tablespoon or half a cup or six inches is when their estimates can actually be far off.

This problem has been magnified in recent decades as serving sizes have grown. Restaurant portions have famously expanded. A "serving" of pasta in a restaurant can easily contain three or four of the outer "portions". Even fruits are bigger, so it used to be a medium sized fruit now looks a little like us.

You will need to measure cups and spoons, a ruler or tape measure and hopefully a scale. Ideally, at this point you will pick up some measuring instruments so you can see exactly what we are talking about.

3 - Non-starchy vegetables

Although non-starchy vegetables have some carbohydrate, they do not have much and the nutritional danger of carb is huge with most of them. On a low carb diet, these vegetables take the place of starch and carb foods, and most people on a low-carb diet end up doubling or tripling the amount of these vegetables they eat. People on moderate-carb diets sometimes don't count them at all.

That said, carb counting in vegetables can be tricky due to irregular shapes and different ways of cutting and cooking. For example, the asparagus skewers range from very thin to as thick as your thumb. A "medium" Bell pepper according to the database may not be what we imagine. Counting carbs in vegetables can be a good time to get out the ruler or tape measure to make sure you know what 4 inches really looks like.

Greens are the lowest vegetables in carbs. Some low-carb plans even count greens as "free foods" as they are low in carbs and surrounded by so many fibers that they don't tend to raise blood sugar - but check your own plan before deciding to do so this.

4 - Counting Carb in Fruit

Fruits have a large variation in how much carbohydrate they contain, from raspberries, at 3.5 grams net carb per half cup, to raisins, at 31 grams for a quarter cup. In general, berries have the least sugar, and tropical and dried fruits have the most.

Fruits tend to be even more irregularly shaped than vegetables, so sometimes you may need to measure. Another problem is that the average size of many fruits has grown over the years. For example, a "medium" banana is approx. 7 inches long. Just try to find a 7-inch. Same with apples - a medium is 3 inches across that most people would think of as small.

5 - Beans and starchy vegetables

If you have a place in your carb allocation, beans and starch vegetables are an excellent choice because they tend to be very nutritious compared to other higher carb foods. In addition, beans have very slowly digested carbohydrate and resistant starch, especially if you strain and cook them yourself instead of buying canned beans.

Half a cup of beans is approx. 15 grams of carb, with the exception of soybeans.

More Bean Info:

Black beans

Chickpeas (Garbanzo Beans)

Lentils

Soybeans

Starchy vegetables vary greatly in how much carb they have. Mashed potatoes are another of these "half a cup is about 15 grams of carb" offerings.

6 - Cereals, including pasta

Note: Eating cereal foods is not a requirement! The American Diabetes Association website says: If you are going to eat cercal, choose the most nutritious. Choose whole grains.

Diabetes educators use 15 grams of carbohydrate as a measure of serving size. For cereals, it is about half a cup of cooked cereal, except rice and pasta, where a serving is 1/3 of a cup.

Check out Carb Counter for:

- Amaranth
- Corn Meal (including grits, polenta and popcorn)
- Oats (including several types of cooked oats)
- Quinoa
- Rice
- Wheat (including flour, bulgur, pasta, etc.)

7 - Baked goods

The only real way to find the amount of carbohydrate in cakes, cakes, pies, breads, etc. is to read the label and pay close attention to the serving size. Some rough estimates based on 15 grams for a serving:

A slice of bread (note that today many loaves have larger slices than the standard size, so be sure to check the label)

- A 6-inch tortilla, flour or corn
- ½ of a biscuit, or a small one (2 inches in diameter)
- ½ of an English muffin
- ¼ of a large bagel
- 1/3 of a large muffin or small muffin (2½ inches across)
- 4-6 biscuits
- 3 vanilla wafers
- 1 small brownie or frosting cake (2 inch square)

8 - Dairy products

One cup of milk has 11-12 grams of carb in it that comes from sugar (lactose) in milk. In almost all other dairy products, some of the lactose is removed, either by fermentation (yogurt, cheese) or because the cream is used more than the milk (heavy cream). Because the bacteria eat the lactose, there may even be less carb in yogurt than the brand says. Of course, when manufacturers start adding sugar (yogurt is the worst), all bets are off.

Example: An ounce of cheese usually has between half a gram and one gram of carbohydrate (though processed cheeses may have more).

9 - Nuts and seeds

Nuts and seeds are good low carbohydrates because they often have many of the same nutrients as whole grains for a fraction of the carbohydrate, plus healthy fats and often more fiber. Other than chestnuts and cashews (which are starch), most nuts and seeds have between two und four grams of net carb per ounce

10 - Everything else

We have now covered the main categories of foods that have carbohydrate in them. Just about everything else should have a nutrition label so you can figure it out for yourself. Mobile apps and pocket carb counting books can also be useful.

Conclusion

The Atkins Diet is not for everyone, that's for sure. But it can be quite successful if you bring discipline and are ready to say goodbye to sugar and carbohydrates. A waiver in this direction is certainly not unhealthy however; you should check yourself for safety regularly medical check if you pull through the diet phases over several months.

Because ultimately you force your body with the ketosis first in a hunger metabolism, which is not intended as a standard. The longer you stay in this unnatural state, the more important it is to keep your health in view by the professional.

While the Atkins Diet is a successful way to lose weight quickly, it should not be a long-term change in diet. With too much fat and protein and too few vegetables, fruits and fiber, this strict low carb diet is anything but balanced and therefore not suitable for a permanent diet. Too high is the risk of health damage and dysfunction.

The Atkins Diet is only suitable for rapid weight loss and as a short-term diet. However, if you are looking for a diet that is also suitable in the longer term, should opt for a diet with a moderate amount of carbohydrates in combination with lots of fresh fiber-rich fruits and vegetables, which is easier to maintain in the long run. Also, vegetable fats such as olive oil should be preferred to animal fats.

Thank You!

Made in the USA
Middletown, DE
13 January 2020